This book is given to:

_____

The Day Before Christmas~

On this _____ *day of* _____

In the year of _____

From: _____

Occasion: _____

The Day Before Christmas

By:

Vivian L. Childs & Mack W. Curry III

CEO: Minister Vivian L. Childs
CFO: Rev/Colonel Dr. Henry Childs (Ret)
COO: Henry Childs II, J.D.
DO: Dr. Ashante Y. Everett
DM: Nakeisha M. Curry, M.D.

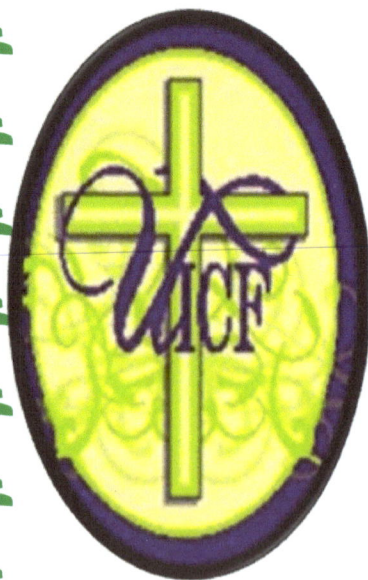

V.L. Childs Publishing
V.L.CHILDS/UICF LLC
P.O. Box 9334
Warner Robins, GA 31095
vlccreations@yahoo.com
www.vivianlchilds.com

First published by V.L. Childs 12/11/2009
ISBN: 978-0-9799896-8-1

Authors: Vivian L. Childs & Mack W. Curry III

Editorial Team: Henry Childs, Henry Childs II, Nakeisha M. Curry, Ashante Y. Everett

Cover/Layout design: Vivian L. Childs

This **book** is dedicated to children everywhere!

It was the day
before Christmas
and all through the
shops,
not a person was
smiling,
unless they were a
tot.

All of the shelves
were empty, not a
thing was in stock,
as we
roamed all about
trying to beat the
clock.

Not that it
mattered,
that all would be
lost,
if we didn't find the
gift,
no matter
the cost.

We pleaded,
they tried,
they offered,
we cried,
as people waited in
line
for a special train
ride.

When out of the
blue,
on that ride just for
two,
I spotted
the thing
that I needed
for you.

It was there
all the time,
I simply needed
to look,
and rush like
thunder,
to grab the last
Book.

How could it be,
what I needed
for me,
was a **Book**
about **Thee**,
to go under
my
tree.

Some
call it luck
but I'm
blessed to say,
that only He
can make it
that special
way.

Sometimes
what we need,
is already here,
if we are willing
to believe,
and not
give in
to fear.

I knew
in a moment,
with no time
to spare,
that tomorrow
would come
and allow
me to

share.

So as I
offer to you,
a measure of cheer,
and pray
that
your life
will be prosperous
next year.

Together
we will,
accomplish
great things,
if we all
remember,
that we are
a team.

So with a prayer
in one hand, and a
desire in the other,
we are truly
destined,
to go
much, much
farther.

So, let's do it!   Go
Trey, go Nakeisha,
and Alyssa too. I
love you all so
much for the things
that you do. Go
Ashante, go
Gordon, go Aralyn,
and Pac.
My love for you all

is sturdier than a rock. Go Henry (H.C.), go Alexis oh dear; go Isabelle, go Victoria, and Maddox with great cheer. Arnetta, my grandbaby too, I'll send you hugs

and kisses till I'm a
hundred and two.
Papa and grandma
(Gran-gran) hold
you all so dear, and
cherish the times
when you are
all here!

HOME
SWEET HOME

So,

with this

Book

as my guide, it

gives me

so much pride,

to be able

to say:

"MERRY

CHRISTMAS

TO

ALL,

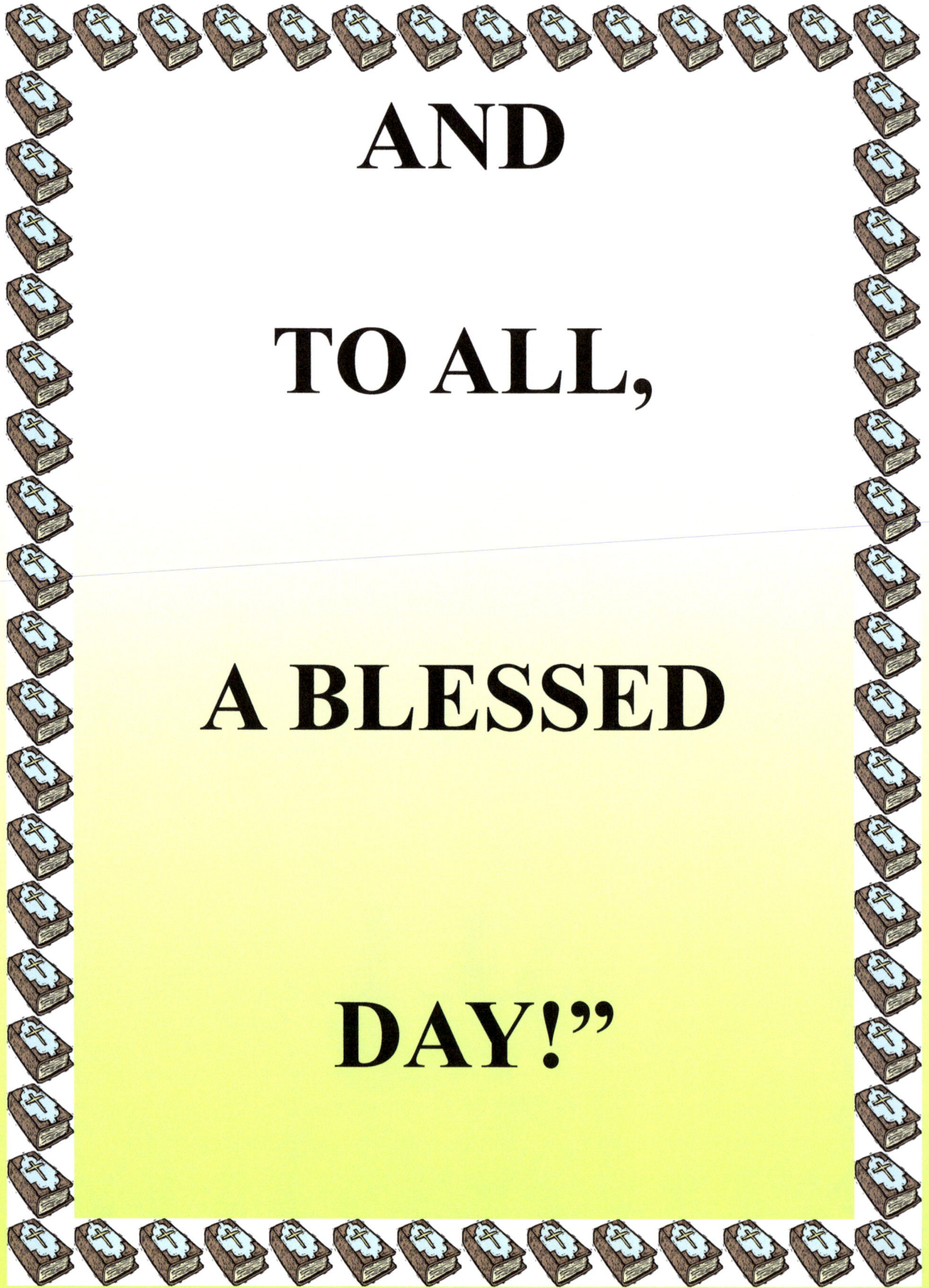

AND

TO ALL,

A BLESSED

DAY!"

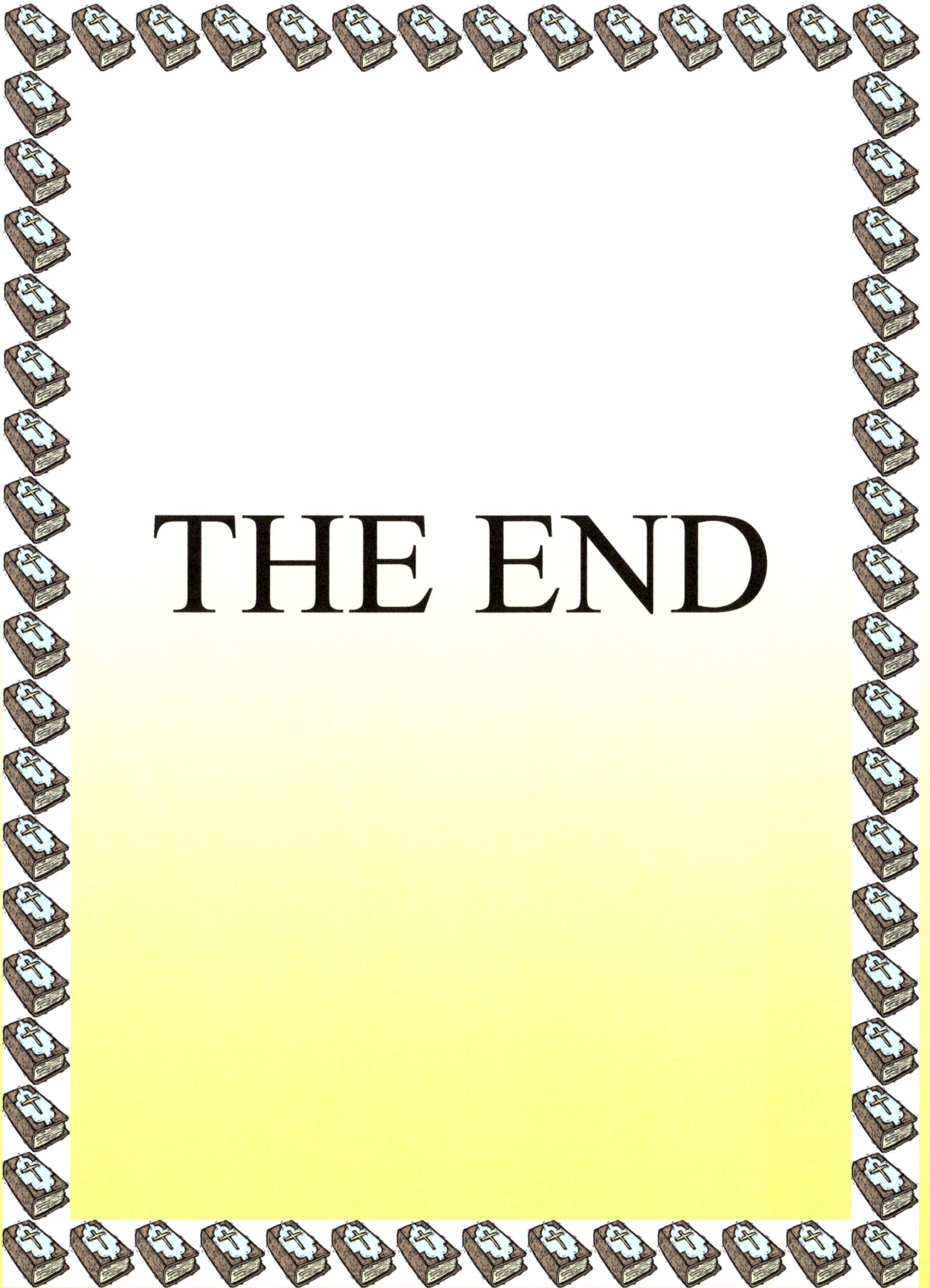

THE END

www.ingramcontent.com/pod-product-compliance
Lightning Source LLC
LaVergne TN
LVHW072120070426
835511LV00002B/44